THE MONASTERY OF BATALHA

THE MONASTERY OF BATALHA

JOSÉ CUSTÓDIO VIEIRA DA SILVA

PEDRO REDOL

SCALA

MINISTÉRIO DA CULTURA

ippar

Instituto Português do
Património Arquitectónico

© Instituto Português do Património Arquitectónico (IPPAR)
and Scala Publishers, 2007

First published in 2007 by Scala Publishers Ltd
Northburgh House
10 Northburgh Street
London EC1V OAT

ISBN-10: 1 85759 382 0
ISBN-13: 978 1 85759 382 2

AUTHORS
José Custódio Vieira da Silva, Pedro Redol
Text translated from the Portuguese by Isabel Varea

EDITORIAL CO-ORDINATION
Manuel Lacerda (DE/IPPAR), Miguel Soromenho (DE/IPPAR),
Sandra Pisano (Scala Publishers)

EDITORIAL ASSISTANCE
Dulce de Freitas Ferraz (DCD/IPPAR)
António Ferreira Gomes (DCD/IPPAR)

PICTURE RESEARCH
Dulce de Freitas Ferraz (DCD/IPPAR)

DESIGN
Nigel Soper

PRINTED in Spain
10 9 8 7 6 5 4 3 2 1

PHOTOGRAPHIC CREDITS
All photographs by Luis Pavão in collaboration with Carlos Sá except:
IPPAR/Henrique Ruas page 107; IPPAR/José Manuel pages 114, 115,
116, 117, 118, 119, 120, 121, 122, 124, 125; IPM/DFF/José Pessoa page 123
Photographic reproduction Henrique Ruas pages 9, 25, 59 top,
65, 74, 85, 106, 110, 115 left; José Augusto Sousa/Photographic Collection –
Museu Vicentes pages 59 bottom, 91

Plan: © IPPAR, Maria João Saldanha/De visu

Previous page
South façade and the Founder's Chapel

CONTENTS

FOREWORD

The Monastery of Batalha is a memorial to the battle that achieved full independence for the Kingdom of Portugal, and later it became home to the royal pantheon of the emerging Avis dynasty. Quite apart from its symbolism, the monastery is one of Portugal's most impressive national monuments. It is, in fact, a unique example of European – not simply Portuguese – Gothic, testifying to the cultural and artistic interaction that took place at the time between the Mediterranean south and the Atlantic north. For this reason UNESCO has rightly named it a World Heritage Site.

Improving conditions for visitors and increasing their understanding of the whole monastic complex at Batalha has been, and continues to be, one of our main concerns in managing the site. This guide, produced in partnership with Scala Publishers, is another essential means of communicating information and enabling the visitor to understand the ideas and intentions of the patrons and architects who created the monument so many centuries ago.

Elísio Summavielle
President of the Instituto Português do Património Arquitectónico (IPPAR)

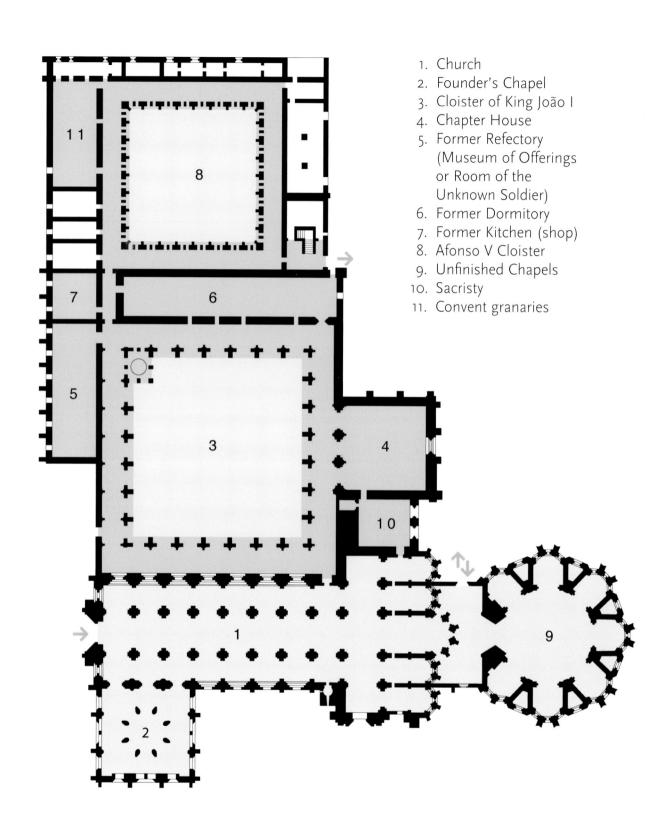

1. Church
2. Founder's Chapel
3. Cloister of King João I
4. Chapter House
5. Former Refectory
   (Museum of Offerings
   or Room of the
   Unknown Soldier)
6. Former Dormitory
7. Former Kitchen (shop)
8. Afonso V Cloister
9. Unfinished Chapels
10. Sacristy
11. Convent granaries

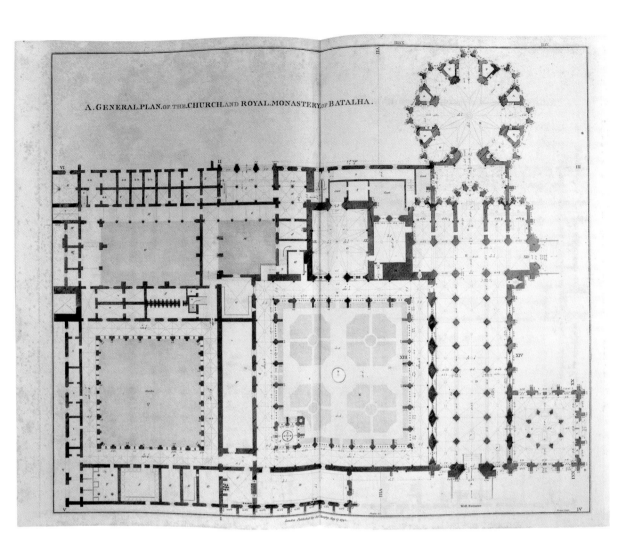

A.GENERAL.PLAN.OF.THE.CHURCH.AND.ROYAL.MONASTERY.OF.BATALHA.

General plan of the
Monastery of Batalha,
including the buildings
on the east side
destroyed during
the 19th-century
restorations, drawing
by James Murphy, 1795
(Biblioteca e Arquivo
Histórico das Obras
Publicas)

THE FOUNDATION OF THE MONASTERY

On 4 October 1426 King João I of Portugal (1357–1433) signed his last will and testament at the Royal Palace at Sintra. It was no coincidence that he chose Sintra as the setting for this important task, as he had always felt a particular fondness for the hilltop palace near Lisbon, which survives to this day. The work he undertook to extend the palace resulted in a series of buildings that have come to occupy an important place in the history of European civil architecture.

As he signed his will in a secluded palace room that day, the king was observing one of the rituals of late-medieval society: to make one's peace with God, oneself and society, both in order to achieve eternal salvation as well as to be remembered with love and respect by one's fellow men.

The will contained many routine clauses common in a legal document of this kind but its most striking feature was the special attention given to a particular building: the Monastery of Batalha, otherwise known as the Monastery of Santa Maria da Vitória. Writing in the first person, the monarch revealed the motives that drove him to construct the building and his reasons for handing it over to the religious community of the Dominicans. He also outlined certain arrangements for supporting the members of this order of mendicant friars, who, once they had moved out of town, would no longer be able to rely on the tenants

General view of
the monastery

West façade of the church, with the Founder's Chapel extending to the right

whose rents helped them to survive. As well as being extremely unusual in a late-medieval will, this detailed explanation indicated the importance the king attached to the monastery he founded.

Part of the document he dictated (quoted here using modern spelling) outlines the process by which the monastery came to be built and subsequently given over to the Dominicans.

'Item: inasmuch as we promised on the day of the battle we fought with the King of Castile, in which Our Lord God granted us victory, to build close to the spot where it occurred a Monastery in honour of Our Lady Saint Mary, the eve of whose feast-day it was; and after it was begun Doctor João das Regras, our chancellor, and Friar Lourenço Lampreia, our confessor, during the siege of Melgaço, did require that we command that it be given to the Order of Saint Dominic and that we should so do in order to fulfil our promise in honour of the aforesaid Saint Mary: and they told us that the Order was devoted to Our Lady and gave the reasons why, and when we heard these we did agree and did command that the Monastery be given to the said Order.'

By the time the will was drawn up, 41 years had passed since 14 August 1385 – the day João I faced the King of Castile's mighty army in the fields of Aljubarrota. Only recently appointed king by the Cortes (or parliament), sitting in Coimbra between March and April of that year, he had until then occupied the position of Master of the Military Order of Avis. Among those supporting his candidacy was Doctor João das Regras (?–1404), a distinguished jurist and professor at the University of Lisbon, who put forward a series of complex arguments to convince the illustrious members of the Cortes that João I was the only contender with the necessary credentials to be crowned King of Portugal.

The Portuguese throne had been vacant since the death of King Fernando on 22 October 1383, and the prospect of the King of Castile, whose wife Beatrice was Fernando's only daughter, claiming his wife's legitimate right to the Portuguese throne had provoked a desperate crisis. After a series of military encounters – some more serious than others – matters came to a head on 14 August 1385. That afternoon at Aljubarrota the Portuguese army, under the command of João I, inflicted a heavy defeat on the much larger and better-equipped Castilian force, obliging the King of Castile to retreat and abandon his hopes

The Royal Cloister, chapter house, north transept and north side of the church

of claiming the Portuguese crown.

On the day of the battle (the eve of the feast of the Assumption of Our Lady), the king, realising how much was at stake, invoked the protection of the Mother of Christ and vowed that he would build a monastery and dedicate it to her if she granted him victory. Following his military success he quickly set about honouring his pledge. The site he chose was not the battlefield itself but a nearby location just to the north, 'level with Canoeira', which fell within the city limits of Leiria. The terrain there was suitable and, above all, there was plenty of water – essential if a community was to settle there. The king acquired the site from its owner, Egas Coelho, a friend and comrade-in-arms. Thus the Monastery of Batalha came into being, as a votive offering to the Virgin Mary.

The significance of the project went far beyond the simple fulfilment of a vow, however. From the outset it symbolised the sanctity of João I as King of Portugal. Indeed the military triumph achieved thanks to the protection of the Virgin Mary ('defender of ourselves and our kingdom', as the king referred to her) was regarded as a sign of divine approval of João I as legitimate ruler, endorsing the earthly approval of the Cortes in Coimbra. Consequently, the monastery became the iconic representation of a new dynasty, personified by João I and legitimised by the will of God.

The religious community finally chosen by the king to occupy the monastery was, as he stated in his will, the Order of St Dominic. However, this may not have been his original intention. It was only after the persistent entreaties of his confessor, the Dominican Friar João Lampreia, and of João das Regras, during the prolonged siege of the northern Portuguese town of Melgaço, that the monarch considered the possibility and gave in to their pleas. In April 1388, the king handed over the crucial deed of gift to the Dominicans, who then took possession of the monastery.

By this time, nearly three years after the victory at Aljubarrota, the building works, financed by taxes levied in Leiria, must have been well under way, a fact that seems to be confirmed by the insistent and wide-ranging arguments put forward by João das Regras and João Lampreia, who would no doubt have been eager to forestall any other ideas the king might be harbouring about who should occupy the

South door of the
church, opening onto
the south transept

monastery. It is worth taking a closer look at the Order to whom the monastic house was finally granted; an examination of the Dominican way of life, viewed from both from a historical as well as an architectural standpoint, sheds light on the thinking of the time and helps to explain why certain building practices were adopted.

The only argument presented by the monarch in his will (and the main reason he hesitated about the handover to the Dominicans) concerned his doubts over the Order's loyalty to the cult of Our Lady, to whom he had vowed to dedicate the monastery. In order to persuade King João to change his mind, either his Dominican confessor or the learned João das Regras repeatedly and insistently tried to convince him that 'the said Order in particular was devoted to Our Lady'. Indeed, since the founding of the Dominican order, its deep devotion to Our Lady, and particularly its promotion of the Rosary, had been among its most defining and identifiable characteristics.

It is thought that the monarch's original intention had been to give the Monastery of Batalha to the Cistercians, a religious community that was distinguished for its deep devotion to the Mother of God and the emphasis it placed on spreading the cult of Mary. The Cistercian Order was famed for the intensely mystical nature of the spoken and written outpourings of its members, among them St Bernard of Clairvaux. As Master of the Military Order of Avis, João I was well acquainted with the Cistercian rule, whose ordinances served as a guide to the military congregation under his command.

A further influence presented itself in the form of the abbot of the Cistercian monastery at Alcobaça, João de Ornelas, who was not only a friend of the king but also his loyal supporter against the King of Castile. The bond between them was strengthened by the fact that João's first son, who died at the age of 10, had been baptised at the monastery. Since Alcobaça was so close to the scene of the battle of Aljubarrota, and because a system was already in place within the Cistercian organisation for forging such links between two monastic houses, it would have made sense to grant the newly founded monastery to the monks of Alcobaça as a token of the king's gratitude for the support of Abbot João de Ornelas. In addition, the Alcobaça monastery was in a strong enough position financially to support the monastery at Batalha, and was also close enough to share facilities with the new house, meaning that the king would not have to donate as many moveable assets or erect as many buildings for the new religious community. Moreover, the monarch made a point of mentioning in his will that he had, with papal approval, purchased a number of properties to ensure the Dominicans' livelihood, presumably well before reaching his final decision to hand the monastery over to them.

A further reason why the monarch might have considered granting the Monastery of Batalha to the Cistercian monks at Alcobaça was the fact that the body of his father, Pedro I (1320–67), rested in the royal pantheon at Alcobaça. Forging such a link would lend greater credibility to his royal lineage, while simultaneously drawing attention away from the fact that he had been born out of wedlock. Indeed, during the early years of his reign, João I had felt a constant need to reaffirm his royal descent in order to justify his hereditary right to the powers bestowed on him by the Cortes in Coimbra. He even ordered the words 'son of King Pedro' to be carved on the helmet above his coat of arms on the south-side door of the monastery church.

Church gargoyle

These reasons support the theory that João I's original plan may have been to grant the new religious house to the monks at Alcobaça. They may also help to explain why the building – which the king helped to design and began to construct, and for which he no doubt provided the finances – does not appear to have included facilities that would have been deemed essential to a mendicant community living far from city life.

In fact, apart from the church and sacristy, initially the building appears to have consisted only of the Royal Cloister, the chapter house, the dormitory, the kitchen and the refectory. This constituted only the most basic arrangement necessary to a monastic community whose principal mission was to worship the Virgin Mary and pray for divine protection. Apart from that, the proximity of the mother-house at Alcobaça made it possible to provide for all the other material and spiritual needs of the Cistercian community that might eventually settle there. The monarch also left instructions in his will that, on the anniversary of his death and that of his queen, the monks of Alcobaça should travel to the Monastery of Batalha in order to join the Dominican community in saying prayers for their souls.

Whatever the king's original intention, he was finally convinced by the case presented by João das Regras and João Lampreia during the long siege of Monção. Along with the Dominicans' devotion to the Virgin Mary (a hallmark of the Order since its foundation), their support in the later fourteenth century of the Pope in Rome, then in Avignon (supported by Castile), must have influenced the king's final decision to grant them the monastery. Furthermore, the Order's leading chronicler in Portugal, Friar Luís de Sousa (1555–1632), made a point of noting that the Dominicans 'made no promises or plans, nor gave any kind of order, because the whole construction of the monastery was the responsibility of the king and those who governed there in his name', suggesting that they left the design and construction of the new monastery entirely to the architects and craftsmen appointed by the monarch.

South transept
of the church

South transept of the
church, showing the
connection between
the south aisle and
the central nave

THE CONSTRUCTION PROCESS
AND THE ARCHITECTS

Although the date that the building works began is uncertain, it is known that a building site large enough for a project of this size was set up a year or two after the Battle of Aljubarrota. The king himself stated in his will that work on the monastery complex had begun at the time of the siege of Melgaço in 1387.

Regardless of the exact date, it is clear that the king rapidly set about fulfilling his pledge of 14 March 1385. At the same time, the sheer architectural scale and artistic brilliance of his cherished project were highly unusual in medieval Portuguese architecture, only the Monastery of Alcobaça bearing any comparison. As well as providing the funds, the king was involved in the huge task of sourcing the best materials and recruiting a team of master craftsmen and a journeyman of sufficient calibre for such a prestigious venture. Moreover, it is known from documents relating to the preparation and functioning of this huge building site that it was organised as efficiently as comparable projects in other parts of Europe. The same source also provides the names of the leading master craftsmen involved.

The first architect was Afonso Domingues, who worked on the monastery from the day building began until 1402, when he is thought to have died. To be chosen by the king to design and oversee this great royal project meant that Domingues must have been a master builder of exceptional merit, possibly the best in Portugal. He drew up the initial overall plan of the monastic complex, which included the church and sacristy, along with the other basic facilities needed for monastic life, namely a chapter house, dormitory, kitchen and refectory. Over the course of almost 14 years Domingues was in charge of the construction of most of the church, the sacristy and two sides of the cloister, as well as making a start on the chapter house.

In 1402 he was succeeded by Huguet, a foreign master builder who had also been working on site at Batalha with Domingues, although not in a supervisory capacity. In the 36 years that he was in charge of operations – from 1402 until his death in 1438 – he completed the work begun by his predecessor, finishing the church, the cloister, the chapter house and other parts of the building. It appears from the will João I drew up in the same year that the church was completed by 1426. While dictating that 'the cloister, living quarters and other buildings necessary to the said Monastery be completed', no mention is made of the church, which may suggest that it had been completed by then. In any case, when Huguet took over, he introduced architectural and decorative innovations that were very different from the rather archaic designs of Domingues. The great vaulted ceiling mounted in a single piece above the chapter house provides the most obvious evidence of this.

Huguet was also responsible for designing the centrally planned Founder's Chapel and the Unfinished Chapels. He completed the former, which João I commissioned to be the eventual site of his own tomb. The latter, commissioned for the same purpose by João's son, King Duarte (1391–1438), were never completed, hence the name by which they are still known today.

The third master builder to take charge of the site was Martim Vasques, whose task between 1438 and 1448 was to complete the parts of the monastery that were started during the regency of Prince Pedro (1392–1449), brother of King Duarte. For this reason he is not credited with making any major structural or artistic contribution to the building.

A more important figure was his nephew, Fernão de Évora, who succeeded his uncle as fourth

architect, a post he held from 1448 to 1477. He presided over the building of the monastery's new cloister, known as the Afonso V Cloister after King Afonso V (1432–81), who financed the project and during whose reign it was built. This second cloister introduced a new formal vocabulary, the austerity of which was in complete contrast to Huguet's flamboyant, exuberant designs.

There followed a period when progress was slow and there seems to have been a rapid turnover of architects. In less than eight years – between 1477 and 1485 – four were appointed, whereas the four previous masters had covered almost a century between them.

The last architect to make a significant contribution to the building of the monastery at Batalha was Mateus Fernandes, who was involved in its construction from 1490 until his death in 1515. He was responsible for the second construction phase of the Unfinished Chapels, under the order of and financed by King Manuel I (1469–1521). Although, like Huguet, Fernandes failed to achieve his objective – because the king later lost interest in the project – he succeeded in leaving his personal stamp on the building, most significantly on the magnificent portal of the Unfinished Chapels, one of the earliest and most original manifestations of Manueline art. He was also responsible for completing the tracery screens in the Royal Cloister, which exemplify the distinctive decorative language of Portuguese art that marked the reign of Manuel I. The clearest demonstration of the social importance he achieved was that he was the only architect permitted to be buried in the church – immediately inside the main entrance – where he lies with his wife under a flat tombstone.

Apart from the aforementioned architects, a succession of master builders oversaw the slow construction of the monastery throughout the fifteenth and sixteenth centuries, their main task being to continue with the work in progress. An interesting consequence of the prolonged operation on the Batalha site was the number of family relationships that were formed. A certain Master Conrate had two daughters, one of whom, Branca Eanes, married the carpenter João de Sintra, while her sister, Catarina Eanes, became the wife of the stained-glass window maker, Master Guilherme. Catarina gave birth to a daughter, Isabel Guilherme, who went on to marry the last architect to make a significant contribution to the building of the monastery, the aforementioned Mateus Fernandes. As for Master Guilherme, although a glazier by trade, he actually took charge of the site in 1480, albeit for a short time. This illustrates not only the esteem in which he was held and how influential he was, but it also indicates how important the craft of creating and installing stained-glass windows was regarded within medieval Portuguese art at this time.

General view of the
Afonso V Cloister

Manueline decorations
in the arcades of the
Royal Cloister

North wing of
the Royal Cloister

Church nave and
side aisles seen
from the chancel

INFLUENCES AND REPERCUSSIONS

The huge dimensions of the monastery at Batalha (which were highly unusual in medieval Portuguese monuments), as well as the architectural qualities and aesthetic innovations that distinguish it, have inspired controversy among Portuguese and foreign art historians, who have debated the influences that shaped its construction. The monastic complex was known and widely discussed among cultured members of European society in the late eighteenth and early nineteenth centuries. Particularly influential were the excellent and previously unpublished plans and elevations produced by James Murphy (1760–1814), an Irish architect and medieval architecture enthusiast with a particular interest in the Gothic. He published a book in instalments between 1792 and 1795 that had immediate repercussions in Great Britain and a direct influence on essayists, historians, scholars and aesthetes of the Romantic school in Portugal during the first half of the nineteenth century. It appealed especially to German art and architectural historians, so much so that a German translation appeared in 1813.

National and international recognition of the importance and originality of the Monastery of Batalha made it the subject of extensive restoration work. These pioneering efforts were in no small part due to King Fernando II (1816–85), who was appalled by the ruinous state of some parts of the building. The high calibre of the work of the first restorer, Luís da Silva Mousinho de Albuquerque, carried out between

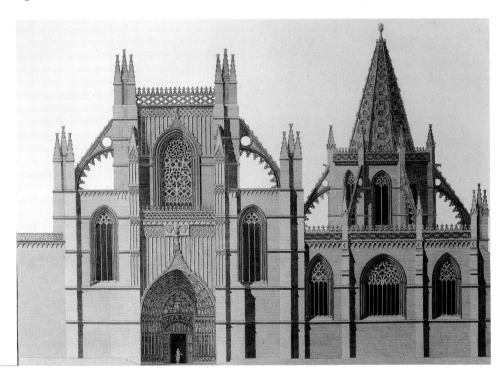

West façade of the church, showing the Founder's Chapel, with James Murphy's proposed spire, drawing by James Murphy, 1795 (Biblioteca e Arquivo Histórico das Obras Publicas)

Central nave
of the church

1840 and 1843, was particularly remarkable, and he admitted that he used the drawings in Murphy's book as an inspiration. Despite this, the restoration efforts resulted in the destruction of several parts of the building. This was, in part, due to the fact that Romantic sensibilities viewed the monastery simply as a historical and nationalistic symbol, dismissing the fact that for several centuries it had been home to a community. In addition to this, the demolished sections (which were part of a cloister that can be traced back to the reign of João III) dated back to the sixteenth century and were not in the Gothic style favoured by the restorers.

Another factor to be considered is that, while the quality of Murphy's drawings were never under dispute, they cannot be assumed to be faithful to the original building. The sketches and elevations that he drew on the spot during a three-week stay in Portugal were later completed in his London studio and

The Founder's Chapel, showing the tomb of João I and Philippa of Lancaster

they embodied an ideal of architectural and artistic perfection that did not correspond to the physical reality of the monastery.

By following Murphy's drawings so closely, Luís da Silva Mousinho de Albuquerque and the restorers who succeeded him may have been responsible for the introduction of formal elements that were alien to the original, in order to lend a certain 'Englishness' to the decoration – something which certain critics were quick to recognise. The fact that João I had married Philippa of Lancaster, daughter of John of Gaunt, Duke of Lancaster, also led some historians to claim that the architect responsible for planning and building the monastery was an Englishman who had accompanied Queen Philippa to Portugal specifically to undertake the task.

There is no doubt that Domingues, the first architect involved in the building of the monastery, was

Portuguese and owned a house in Lisbon in the parish of the Madalena. He was familiar with the work on Lisbon's Romanesque cathedral, which was commissioned by King Afonso IV (1291–1357), who had ordered a Gothic apse, ambulatory and radiating chapels at the eastern end, in a project which used a formal and aesthetic language to rival the best cathedral architecture anywhere in contemporary Europe. Lisbon Cathedral was also groundbreaking within the context of Portuguese Gothic architecture; only the Cistercian monastery at Alcobaça, begun in 1178, is of a similar structure. The art historian Mário Tavares Chicó (1905–66) even remarked that the east end of the cathedral represented the only attempt in Portugal to achieve the grandeur of the great Gothic churches of northern Europe.

It is also thought that Portugal's most outstanding example of late fourteenth-century architecture – the upper choir of the church of São Francisco in Santarém –, erected by order of King Fernando I (1345–1383) to house his tomb, may also have been the work of Domingues. Indeed, the formal and decorative solutions he employed at the Monastery of Batalha closely follow some of the most striking features of both Lisbon Cathedral and the church at Santarém. At the same time, they display some examples of the somewhat archaic vocabulary that was a feature of medieval Portuguese art.

It is known that Huguet, the second architect to take charge at Batalha, was a foreigner, but his precise origins remain unknown. Various historians have argued more or less convincingly that he could have been English, French or Catalan. What is clear is that his contributions to the monastic complex speak of

Masks and foliage
adorning the capitals
of one of the windows
at the entrance to the
chapter house

Following page
The Founder's Chapel,
showing ambulatories
and the central octagon

a master builder who was familiar with the characteristic Late Gothic techniques that were in use across Europe at the time. From the typically flamboyant decorations that adorn the monastery's capitals, pinnacles and turrets, to the spectacular stellar vaults, his elegant artistry have left an indelible mark on the building. He was innovative in the methods he employed, while respecting the structural and decorative elements that had been put in place by the first architect, thus creating a harmony that is evident practically everywhere in the complex.

It is safe to conclude, therefore, that the Late Gothic style made its first appearance in Portugal at the Monastery of Batalha, under the direction of Master Huguet, and spread from there to much of the rest of the country. The master stonemasons, carpenters and simple craftsmen who were trained on the vast construction site, and employed for many years at Batalha, also worked on various other projects and sites, so spreading the new style of art. These influences are clearly evident at the Graça church in Santarém, the Carmelite Church in Lisbon, Guarda and Silves Cathedrals, the Church of the Conception in Beja and the castle at Porto de Mós. And, as the archaeologist and art historian Vergílio Correia (1888–1944) affirmed, the site at Batalha set the standard for Portuguese craftsmen until the second quarter of the sixteenth century.

Curiously, the fourth architect, Fernão de Évora, adopted a formula that stood in marked opposition to the ornate decoration and structural innovation of Huguet. The architectural and decorative language

The vault of the chapter house

he devised for the Afonso V Cloister was sober and austere, with no concession to any decoration apart from a few discreet heraldic emblems on some of the keystones on the vaulting at ground level. The stark contrast between these two artistic interpretations, made more pronounced by their juxtaposition, says much about the often contradictory sensibilities of the late Middle Ages. Fortunately, the Monastery of Batalha is a felicitous blend of two contrasting styles, which is one of the reasons it played such a pivotal role in the architecture of the fifteenth century.

The arrival of Huguet at the site of Batalha, therefore, heralded the Late Gothic style in Portugal, which came to consist of two parallel and contradictory elements. In the first there was clear evidence of the influence of northern Europe, where these ideas had originated; priority was given to the ogee arch and lavish ornamentation that drew on the characteristic vocabulary of the end of the Gothic period. The second, seen in Fernão de Évora's work in the Afonso V Cloister, favoured structural and decorative simplicity, with geometric solutions and clearly defined volumes echoing the Mediterranean sensibility, of which there are clear examples in Catalonia and southern France.

Two powerful currents, the flamboyant Gothic of northern Europe and the unadorned Gothic of the southern Mediterranean, would continue to come together in Portugal well beyond the late- Gothic period. Both were tested for the first time at the Monastery of Batalha, in a pioneering project that would be emulated all over the country.

The upper gallery of
the Afonso V Cloister

The stellar vault above the central octagon in the Founder's Chapel

THE CHURCH

THE EXTERIOR

The sheer size of the monastery's church, with dimensions virtually unheard of in medieval Portuguese architecture (over 80 metres long, 22 metres wide and around 35 metres high) is enough to confirm the importance with which João I regarded the monastery. The church is situated on low ground, which means that the scale of the building is not immediately evident as one approaches it along the Leiria-Lisbon road. On nearing the building, however, the sheer size of it becomes clear and individual technical and artistic details can be picked out. In the soft light of the late afternoon sun the limestone from the nearby quarries is completely transformed and the building resembles a magnificent golden casket.

The church, designed by Domingues, is built on a Latin Cross ground plan, the longest arm consisting of a nave and two side aisles with eight bays, with the nave higher and wider than the aisles on either side. The shorter arms (or transepts) are also remarkable for their size, as they soar to the same height as the nave. The east end of the church consists of five polygonal chapels. The middle one (the chancel) is higher and deeper than the others, which are all of equal size.

The exterior illustrates elements of the groundbreaking decorative scheme introduced by Huguet,

General view of
the church

Detail of a
buttress turret on
the central section
of the church façade

Aerial view of
the monastery

the details of which provide some of the defining images of the building. Among the characteristic Late Gothic features that were seen here for the first time in Portugal is the stone lacework of the balustrades along the top of the walls, the crockets (or curled leaf ornaments) on the pyramidal pinnacles, the ogee arch over the portal, the great window on the main façade and the ornate window tracery in the church and the Founder's Chapel.

A significant feature is the moulding that runs evenly and continuously along all of the church walls at different levels, emphasising the horizontality of the building. The effect is made more dramatic by the use of a straight gable above the tripartite structure of the main façade. Even the vertical lines of the buttresses topped with pinnacles do little to disturb the predominantly horizontal line of the exterior, which culminates in the flat roof of the church. These features, claimed by some historians to be the result of strong English influences in the monastery's construction, are more probably linked to the Mediterranean influences that were being felt across the Iberian Peninsula at the time. A striking example of this are the external walls of the Cathedral of Palma de Mallorca, which are a riot of repetitive horizontal mouldings. Meanwhile, the flat roof is a recurrent feature in southern Europe, historically regarded as a response to climatic conditions. Even in Portugal, before building began at Batalha, the same method was used at Évora Cathedral, which was started in the second half of the thirteenth century. Overall, the external appearance of the church is more akin to Mediterranean Gothic, where differing volumes are combined and horizontal lines are predominant – from the vaults to the extradoses (outer surfaces) of the nave arcades – despite the presence of slender buttresses and walls split vertically by windows.

The flying buttresses above the side aisles, visible from the exterior, proclaim the presence of the vaulted ceiling above the entire body of the church, another innovation that was introduced at Batalha. Such structures were rare in Gothic architecture in Portugal, as church architects usually opted for wooden ceilings. In cases where the naves were covered by stone vaults, the side aisles and naves were kept to the same height to avoid having to use flying buttresses. This was the case at the Cistercian Monastery of Alcobaça (where flying buttresses made their first appearance in Portugal, albeit limited to the east end of the church) and at the Franciscan Monastery of Santa Clara a Velha in Coimbra, which dates from the first half of the fourteenth century.

Following page
South façade of the
Founder's Chapel

Limestone-tiled roof
of the church nave
and transept

The roof of the south
aisle of the church

Terrace and buttresses
above the south aisle
of the church

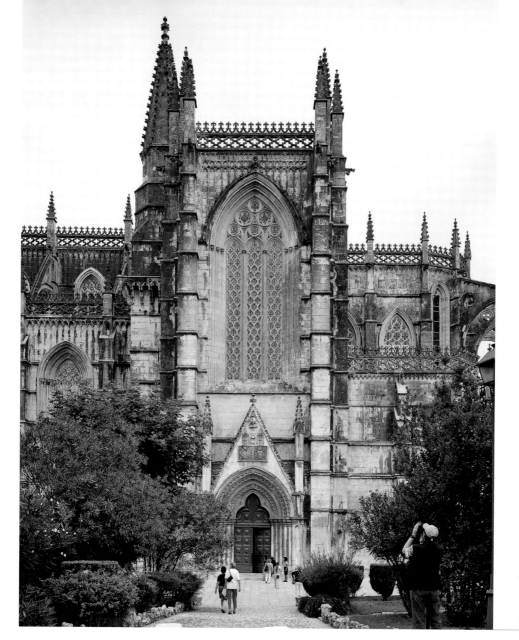

South elevation of the transept of the church, showing the differences in style between Domingues's portal and Huguet's great window

THE SOUTH DOOR

When compared to the west-facing main door, the door in the south transept is an excellent illustration of the different vocabularies employed by the two first architects who worked on the monastery. The archaic style of Domingues's south door contrasts dramatically with the more modern rendition of the west door by Huguet.

The south portal is composed of four archivolts with broken arches; the two outer ones are adorned with small horseshoe arches, the innermost one with a zigzag motif, and the one in between with simple bead moulding. There is no tympanum and the door itself is an elegant trefoil with interwoven mouldings. In contrast to these rather dry, geometric decorations the capitals display two rows of delicately carved and naturalistic foliage, with stalks trailing down like vines between the columns.

Above the arches surrounding the door is a sharply pointed pediment flanked by two tall, pinnacled buttresses. These underscore the autonomy of the portal, which stands away from the adjoining walls in a position that lends it greater structural depth.

The decoration on both the archivolts and the sharply pointed pediment is rooted in ancient Portuguese tradition, the features of which are equally common in other regions of the Iberian Peninsula. The south door provides further confirmation that Domingues's work was inspired by architectural styles of the past.

The south door of the church

Capitals decorated
with plant motifs
at the south door
of the church

The most novel features of the south entrance to the church are the delicately carved coats of arms of the monastery's founders that appear on the pediment. At its centre is the full coat of arms of Portugal, with shield, helmet, crown and plume. Above that, set in quatrefoils and surrounded by rectangular frames, are the armorial bearings of the king and his queen, Philippa of Lancaster, protected by elegant canopies that are in themselves exquisite pieces of micro-architecture.

There are two significant factors relating to the decoration on the door: firstly, the eye-catching decorative motif consists of a heraldic composition representing the king and queen, and, secondly, it is of note that the ornament is entirely secular, considering it adorns the doorway of a church.

João I was greatly interested in heraldry (the study of armorial bearings and noble lineage). Amid the upheaval of the crisis of 1383–85, which culminated in the Battle of Aljubarrota, many of the ancient noble houses in the kingdom were superseded by others that were founded later. As a result of this the king imposed strict rules governing the use of heraldic display, in order to avoid abuses. To administer the rules he appointed a King of Arms, whose task it was to oversee the granting of new coats of arms and to safeguard those already in existence. Some scholars have convincingly argued that these events marked the birth of the science of heraldry in Portugal. The careful positioning on the south door of the church of the coats of arms of João I and Philippa of Lancaster, surmounted by the arms of Portugal, is evidence of the monarch's close interest in the laws of heraldry.

The heraldic elements that recur across the monastery add support to the claim by some art historians that the Monastery of Batalha is the monument that best captures the spirit of the fifteenth century (a golden age of Portuguese heraldic art), and also confirms the crucial role João I played in drawing up and implementing the relevant rules.

The coats of arms that appear in abundance all over the monastery – on the south and main door, in the chancel, the chapter house, the Founder's Chapel and elsewhere – inform us of the people who bore them and make an effective and eloquent statement about the power they exerted. Heraldic displays were among the most significant forms of decoration in the Late Gothic period, either used alone or alongside sacred signs and symbols, which lent them an air of sanctity (as in those on the south door of the church). Clergy and lay people alike were drawn to the new wave of spirituality that swept across Europe at the close of the Middle Ages. The wishes of noble families to see their heraldic devices displayed in churches testified to the renewed religious zeal of the laity. At the same time it announced the presence of lay benefactors within the religious sphere. This phenomenon can be compared to the way in which many paintings and altarpieces at this time depicted both secular and holy figures at prayer in religious scenes, each portrayed in similar detail. This was a sign of one of the most profound intellectual changes to occur in late-medieval Europe.

Heraldic composition
on the pediment of
the south door
of the church

THE MAIN DOOR

The main door is the antithesis of the south, firstly in that it is set into the wall and fits harmoniously into the façade of which it forms a part, unlike the south door, which projects from the wall in a way that disconnects it from the transept. Secondly, although its formal elements constitute a contemporary interpretation of the Late Gothic style, the iconography used had not been seen before in medieval Portuguese art.

The main façade of the church consists of three sections of varying size. The middle section matches the internal structure, where the central nave is higher and wider than the aisles on either side of it. The three sections are marked out by the introduction of buttresses – supporting elements whose verticality is underscored by pyramid-shaped pinnacles decorated with crockets. In the middle section, where the buttresses are duplicated, any impression of heaviness or density that might have resulted has been cleverly avoided by extending the lacy balustrades beyond the blind arcades above the door and the great central window as far as the two tallest buttresses. This solution not only creates an impression of lightness but also increases the visual impact of the central section of the façade.

Even so, the rhythm of the buttresses is not sufficient to render the lines of the main façade predominantly vertical. The lines of force which truly dictate its structure and give it its visual appeal are largely horizontal, either in the form of mouldings which break up the regular rhythm of the façade (and all the other external walls of the church), or through the use of straight gables to top the three sections. Moreover, the delicate open stonework along the top of the walls, and the introduction of the same feature to achieve the total separation of the main door and the large, slightly recessed window above it, reinforce the horizontal lines which together create one of the most dramatic and defining images of the building. Bell towers, which may have lent the building greater verticality, were never included in the plans because it was conceived as a monastic church and bell towers were traditionally seen as the preserve of cathedrals.

Main façade of the church, with the Founder's Chapel on the right and the Royal Cloister on the left

Main façade of the church, with the south wall of the refectory on the far left

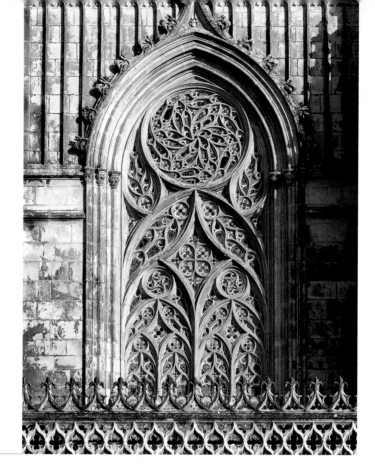

Window in the central section of the main façade of the church

The overall appearance of the monastery façade has a precedent in the Convent of Leça do Balio, near Oporto, whose church was built in the first half of the fourteenth century from beautiful granite ashlar, and is one of the finest and most original pieces of religious Gothic architecture in Portugal. The main façade, belonging to the military and religious order of the Knights Hospitaller (also known as the Knights of Malta) is also constructed in three parts. The side sections end in straight gables topped by conical battlements, while the middle section is cut in half by a protruding balcony. This feature is repeated in the same form and serves the same purpose at the church at Batalha. Apart from its more lavish decoration, perhaps the most striking difference between the church at Batalha and that at Leça do Balio is that Batalha has no rose window marking the second storey of the middle section.

The solution opted for at Batalha is, in fact, highly original. Huguet, almost certainly the architect responsible for completing this part of the building, chose one of the most characteristic architectural features of the Late Gothic period. He designed a large window framed on the outside by an ogee arch which, together with the similar arch surrounding the main door directly below, was one of the first of its kind to be used in Portugal. The dynamic design of this 'pseudo rose window' is in stark contrast to the quiet linearity of the vertical blind arcade and the horizontal moulding on the rest of the façade. A similar but rather more subtle example is the rose window on the main façade of the Graça church at Santarém, where construction began almost simultaneously with Batalha.

Huguet's main door is, of course, much taller, extending nearly halfway up the façade. It is also broader, taking up the entire width of the nave. Its highly sophisticated iconographic scheme was the most complete to have yet been developed in Portuguese Gothic art and rivalled the most advanced examples of the carving and statuary that were a traditional feature of European cathedral entrances. It is not surprising that Virgílio Correia, one of Portugal's leading art historians of the twentieth century, compared it to the original west front of the Cathedral of Santiago de Compostela in northern Spain. He described it as Portugal's 'own Pórtico de la Gloria', and the most complete, the most beautiful and the most pure fusion of architecture and sculpture of the Portuguese Middle Ages, remarkable for its elegant outlines, slender proportions, decorative arrangement and the skill of its stone-carvers.

On either side of the entrance, beneath elegantly carved canopies, the Twelve Apostles are arranged

Main door of the church

on elaborately detailed corbels. In the absence of the usual columns, which are replaced here by slender colonnettes that are more decorative than structural, these upholders of the faith and symbolic pillars of the Church provide actual structural support to the doorway.

Above the Twelve Apostles, occupying the portal's six archivolts and organised hierarchically from the edge towards the centre, stands a collection of figures representing the Kingdom of Heaven. The first two archivolts contain figures from the New Testament. The outermost one features virgins, female saints and martyrs, described by Correia as sitting with great dignity on footstools – suitably coiffed and richly clad – clutching the emblems of their martyrdom. In the second are the standing figures of popes, bishops, deacons, monks and male martyrs, each representing virtue, wisdom and piety, and setting an example to Christians entering the church.

The next two archivolts are devoted to Old Testament figures. Firstly, seated like the virgins and female martyrs, are the Kings of Judah, forebears of the Virgin Mary and hence of the same lineage as Christ himself. Then, taking the same pose as the popes and bishops are the prophets and patriarchs whose teachings and example paved the way for the New Testament.

The two archivolts closest to the tympanum are occupied by angelic figures. The first contains seated angels playing musical instruments, and the second holds standing figures of seraphim with three pairs

Row of apostles on the left of the main door of the church

Tympanum and
archivolts above the
main door of the church

of wings each. The former group is seen to celebrate the approach of God to the throne by playing soft music associated with heavenly bliss. The latter are, according to Saint Dionysius, the Areopagite's hierarchy of angels – the ones closest to the Divinity.

The particular rendering of these figures, and the way they follow the movement of the broken arches of the respective archivolts, is subtly underlined by the fact that each series of figures is presented alternately standing or seated.

The figure of God appears in the tympanum, dominating this magnificent composition. In the centre, seated on a splendid throne covered by an equally impressive canopy, God is portrayed as an old man. His right hand is raised in a gesture of authority and his left hand rests on the globe, accentuating his regal bearing. Beside him are seated the Four Evangelists, reading or annotating books resting on writing desks (except in the case of St Matthew, whose book is held by an angel). Each one is accompanied by the animal that symbolises him in the so-called Tetramorph – the union of the attributes of the Four Evangelists – described in the Book of Revelation. St Mark is represented by a lion, St Luke by an ox, St Matthew by a winged man and St John by an eagle in flight.

Above this imposing group is an arrangement of the Coronation of the Virgin as Queen of Heaven, placed above the last archivolt in the space created by the outline of the ogee arch. Seated on a simple stool, Christ places a crown on his mother's head as she kneels reverently with her hands joined. The significance of this exchange is emphasised by the presence of an impressive canopy – a beautifully executed piece of mini-architecture.

Placed symmetrically at the top of the ogee arch are the same coats of arms of João I and Philippa of Lancaster as appear above the southern entrance. As with the latter, these are set in quatrefoils and surrounded by rectangular frames. In the corners of the rectangles four angels support the coats of arms.

The main portal of the monastery church is worthy of note for a number of reasons. Firstly, the carvings on the pillars, tympanum and archivolts are copies that were made during the nineteenth-century restorations. The originals, which are in various states of disrepair, are on display inside the monastery. Correia, pointing out the finer points of these carved figures, described them by saying that despite being

Kings and prophets
on the archivolts of the
main door of the church

Archivolts of the main
door of the church

imprisoned in garments of heavy cloth falling into many angular folds, the statues remain animated, graceful and refined, often with charming countenances.

The stone-carvers who created the prophets, kings, angels and seraphim achieved a considerable artistry, especially in the variety of facial expressions they created. The iconography produced and the aesthetic values observed at Batalha through the work of its stone-carvers and sculptors both directly and indirectly influenced Portuguese sculpture throughout the fifteenth century.

The main portal is also of note in that the iconographic layout is rather unusual. One example of this is the sequence in which the figures in the archivolts appear: virgins, martyrs and New Testament saints are situated on the outer edge, with Old Testament prophets and kings in the two middle archivolts, before the angels and seraphim. A more logical sequence would place these two latter groups in the outermost archivolts, since they are 'ancient' figures who historically announced and prepared for the coming of

Tympanum above the main door of the church

Saint Luke the Evangelist, original relief taken from the tympanum above the main door of the church

The Coronation of our
Lady, above the main
door of the church

Christ's kingdom. Following this hierarchical arrangement, the New Testament figures would appear in
the innermost archivolts.

On the tympanum the Four Evangelists and their attributes are also configured in an unusual way. At
the top, to the right of Christ, are St John and the eagle; on the left is St Matthew with the angel; at the
bottom right, St Luke sits with the ox, with St Mark and the lion on the left. In line with the rules of
symbolism followed in the Middle Ages, St Matthew would normally appear at the top, to the right of
Christ, with St John on the left. Below, to the right, would be St Mark, with St Luke to the left. This
configuration, presented simultaneously with the Four Evangelists and the Tetramorph, was not unknown
but neither was it common.

In the most common representation of Christ in both Romanesque and Gothic art, He is shown
holding the Book of Life. The tympanum of the monastery church at Batalha, however, shows Christ
portrayed as an old man seated majestically on a throne, with a sphere representing the world resting
safely beneath his right hand.

This somewhat unusual depiction of Christ, equipped with the symbols of imperial authority, can be
seen to carry the same message that is conveyed in the imagery of the entire portal. The corbels that
support the Apostles Peter and Paul illustrate, once again, the coats of arms of João I and Philippa of
Lancaster. In this way, an association is made between the two great champions and pillars of the church,
and the king and queen, expressed in the language of heraldry. The king and queen of Portugal, as the
founders and creators of a new dynasty, become legitimised by this sanctification, hence their power to
govern mirrors the power of God himself. They would have seen it as right and fitting, therefore, that an
image of imperial authority be placed at the centre of the tympanum, at the threshold to the church.

Coats of arms of
João I and Philippa of
Lancaster above the
main door of the church

Saint Bartholomew
the Apostle, original
sculpture taken from
the main portal of
the church

Saint Bartholomew
the Apostle, 19th-
century copy on the
main portal of the
church

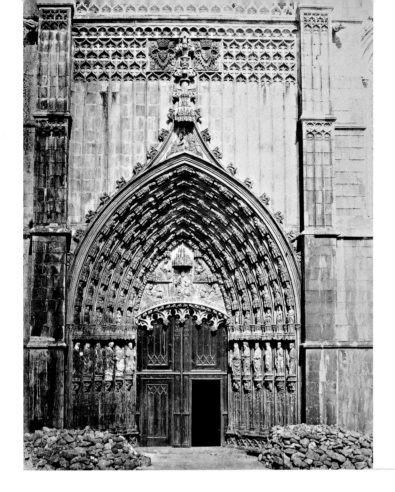

Main door of the
church, photograph
by Vigé and Plessix,
19th century
(Biblioteca da Ajuda)

Main door of the church
showing the work of the
19th-century restorers,
photograph by Joaquim
Augusto Sousa
(Museu Vicentes)

The King of Judah, original sculpture from the main portal of the church, removed during the 19th-century restorations

Seraph, original sculpture from the main portal of the church, removed during the 19th-century restorations

Main door of the church

Church nave

Multicoloured
reflections on the pillars
of the church nave

THE INTERIOR

What is immediately striking on entering the church is the sheer majesty and grandeur of its interior. The astounding verticality of the nave contrasts dramatically with the distinctive horizontal lines that dominate the exterior. This verticality is intensified by the closely aligned pillars supporting the vaulted ceiling, which draw the eye straight to the chancel. The interplay between the pale and perfectly rectangular-cut stone, which so impressed the great chronicler of the Dominican Order, Friar Luís de Sousa (1555–1632), and the luminous colours of the windows still produce the same mystical effect that the subdued light and bright colours projected into the church by the windows would have done in the past. The clever and controlled use of lighting is one of the factors that accentuates the serene splendour of the interior of this building.

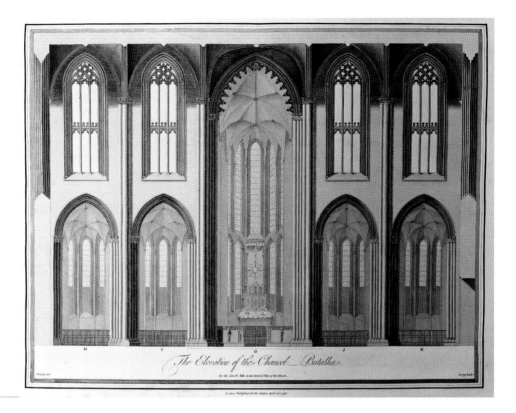

The Elevation of the Chancel — Batalha

Elevation of the chapels
at the east end of the
church, drawing by
James Murphy, 1795
(Biblioteca e Arquivo
Histórico das Obras
Publicas)

The nave consists of a two-storey elevation, comprising nave arcades and a clerestory formed by wide windows of three lights each. The polystyle pillars supporting the vault are set so closely together that they seem to form a wall, which adds to the verticality of the space. In addition to this, the absence of any horizontal moulding on the pillars along the nave helps to create a sensation of height, which is not lessened by the thickness of the pillars or the density of the pendentives.

The vaults above the nave and those above the side aisles are ribbed with ogees and buttresses, with large bosses decorated in highly naturalistic plant motifs. Those above the nave are particularly impressive, not only for their plant designs but also for their unusual size, a detail suggesting that Huguet may have been responsible for adding the finishing touches to the ceiling.

The two side aisles are lower and narrower than the nave but they are lit in the same way – by wide, three-light windows. The vaulting above them, which is at the same high level as the nave arcade, creates a sense of spatial continuity and a subtle interplay with the thick wall of pillars. These architectural techniques, whilst challenging our perception of space, are also responsible for the dynamic relationship between width and height, intensifying the contrast between the horizontality that dominates the exterior of the church and the intense verticality of its interior.

The architectural design of the nave and side aisles of the church was the work of Domingues. His plan respects the traditions of Portuguese Gothic architecture, most notably in its omission of a triforium (or gallery above the arcade) and the resulting two-storey elevation. The architect's biggest challenge was to build a vaulted roof over the entire church – a very unusual feature in Portuguese Gothic architecture. He made use of time-honoured methods to solve the problems he encountered, such as using a type of pillar that had been introduced in the thirteenth century at Évora Cathedral. The same method was used during the fourteenth century in other buildings, where the pendentives clearly show the influence of the Monastery of Alcobaça.

The east end of the church consists of five polygonal chapels preceded by rectangular bays, the middle one of which is higher and deeper than the other four, which are all of the same height and depth. In this part of the church, where building first began, Domingues applied more modern solutions than those

used in the nave and side aisles, based on the experience he had gained while working on the east end of Lisbon Cathedral. The art historian Mário Tavares Chicó first drew attention to this fact; according to his theory, since the apses in the church at Batalha were the first of their kind in Portugal, it would be fair to assume that when Domingues drew up his plans, he simply reproduced the ambulatory chapels at Lisbon Cathedral. The only difference is that he appears to have altered the proportions (which are more elegant here) and to have added, as a finishing touch, certain details similar to those in the choir at the Monastery of São Francisco in Santarém, built during the reign of King Fernando.

The two-storey elevation of the chancel was an innovation in Portuguese Gothic architecture. Its great height (the same as the nave) accentuates the nave's depth and lends luminosity and translucence to

Vaulted ceiling above the chancel of the church

Windows on the second storey of the chancel

the east end of the church. Although Domingues may have been credited with these ideas, it was Huguet who raised the chancel to the same level as the nave, decorating the arch with a delicate lace edge and building a type of roof that was previously unknown in Portugal.

All the side chapels at the east end, which are linked by the narrow arches commonly found in mendicant churches, and which open directly onto the transept, have been identified by Luís de Sousa. The first, next to the sacristy, was dedicated to St Barbara, the second to Our Lady of the Rosary, and the third, on the right of the chancel, to Our Lady of Mercy. The fourth chapel is known only for the tomb that rests there, belonging to the Master of the Order of Christ, Lopo Dias de Sousa.

Although the dominant form of decoration used on the capitals and ceiling bosses consists of plant motifs, various others are used, especially on the more elaborately carved capitals. One of these is the motif consisting of figures from the scene of the Annunciation, which appears in the St Barbara chapel, in the nave next to the transept, and again at the entrance to the chapter house. It is a theme particularly dear to devotees of the Virgin Mary, to whom the monastery is dedicated. Another interesting piece of iconography is the configuration on one of the columns in the nave of fifteen angels playing various musical instruments. Like their counterparts on the archivolts of the portal, they evoke an atmosphere of

heavenly angel choirs. They also symbolise the cloistered life of the monastery, where singing the liturgy and chanting the canonical hours are seen to offer a foretaste of Paradise. The archaic style of these images seems to suggest the hand of Domingues, the monastery's first architect.

In addition to these, the painted coats of arms of João I and Philippa of Lancaster in the vaulting above the chancel, as well as the painting of the Portuguese coat of arms supported by an angel on the ceiling of the sacristy, provide more evidence of the almost obsessive use of heraldic emblems by the patrons and founders of the monastery. The positioning of these emblems in the church's most sacred areas confirms the degree to which the laity were involved in religious affairs. At Batalha this phenomenon is most evident in the chancel of the church, where the stained-glass windows (commissioned around 1514) and the lavish altarpiece show King Manuel I (1469–1521) and Queen Maria (1482–1517) kneeling in prayer, accompanied by their children and by two Dominican saints who act as mediators between the royal family and God.

Angel musicians
on capitals in the
north aisle

Detail of the
vaulted ceiling
above the chancel

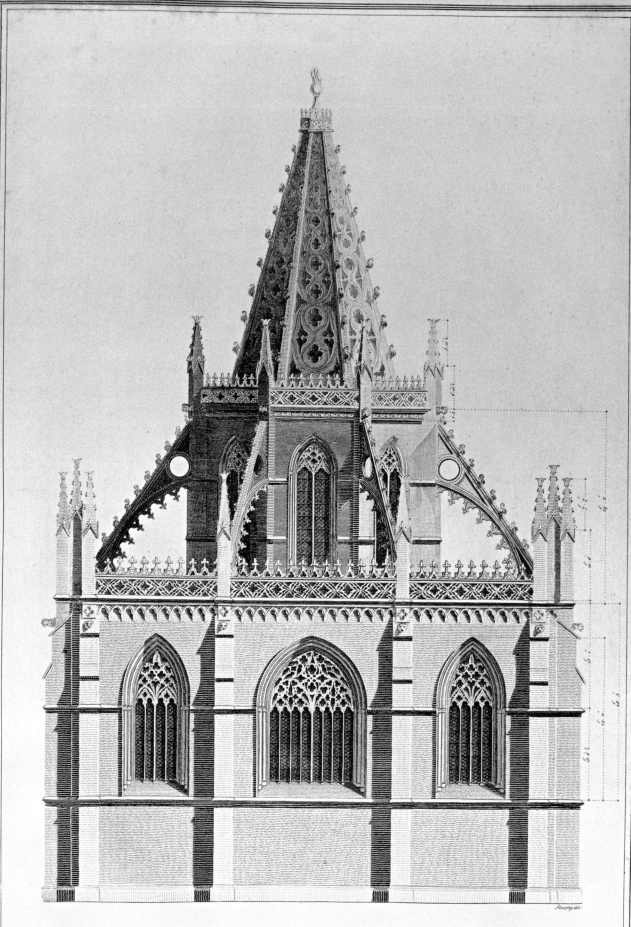

THE **SOUTH ELEVATION** OF THE **MAUSOLEUM** OF **KING JOHN** I.ˢᵗ AT **BATALHA**.

Nᵒ: The Pyramid which formerly crowned this building, was thrown down by the great Earthquake of the year 1755, it is here restored from an old painting, on one of the Windows of the Church.

THE FOUNDER'S CHAPEL

To the right of the church's main façade, and extending along three bays, stands a square chapel, which enhances the horizontal effect of the exterior of the church. If James Murphy's proposals for the renovation of this chapel had been accepted, the results may have been very different. He envisaged replacing the grandiose pinnacle that had previously adorned the roof, which would have given the chapel a vertical projection that it lacks today.

The construction of the chapel, which was not indicated in the initial plans for the monastery, was a late decision by João I, and is referred to in considerable detail in his will of 1426. At that time the monarch resolved that his body should be buried next to the queen, who had been laid to rest in the chancel or, 'once it is finished, in the chapel which I have ordered to be made'. This suggests that work on the chapel was already in progress at this time. In 1434, one year after the king's death, it had been completed, and the royal couple's remains were laid to rest there, fulfilling the wishes of the king.

The Founder's Chapel is interesting in that it was built specifically to house a tomb. It was the first time that a Portuguese monarch had ordered the construction of an independent and personalised space

Western elevation of
the Founder's Chapel

(albeit attached to a monastery church) to serve as a pantheon for members of a dynasty. Indeed, João I expressly forbade the burial there, either in a tall chest tomb like the one he shared with his queen, or under the floor, of anyone 'unless he be King of these realms'. Similarly, the tombs in the chapel walls were reserved for the children and grandchildren of the kings of Portugal. With these conditions in place, the Founder's Chapel became the ultimate expression of the symbolic significance of the Monastery of Batalha. It began as a votive offering in fulfilment of a promise made at Aljubarrota and then, through the presence of an exclusively royal pantheon, became a celebration of the new dynasty founded by King João I.

Huguet was responsible for the planning and construction of the Founder's Chapel, using as a template the English models adopted mainly for the chapter houses that were becoming fairly widespread across Europe at that time. The square floor plan gives way to a central octagon, which is marked out by eight piers and opens out into broken, stilted arches whose delicately carved edging retains much of the original paintwork. The second storey of the octagon is surmounted by a stellar vault on whose central boss is another coat of arms of João I. Soaring above the royal tomb in the centre of the chapel, the vault resembles a canopy of state raised in honour of the king and queen.

Effigies of João I and Philippa of Lancaster lie side by side on top of the huge chest tomb, their crowned heads resting on cushions and their right hands affectionately joined. The king wears a full suit of armour and, over it, a surcoat bearing the royal Portuguese emblems: a shield and castles. In his left hand he

holds a baton of command. The queen, her hair falling in soft waves beneath her crown, is wrapped in a long garment with deep folds, and she clutches a closed Book of Hours in her right hand. Both rest their feet on corbels of natural foliage and their heads are protected by large, meticulously carved canopies displaying their respective coats of arms. The sculptor has achieved a high degree of realism here, especially noticeable in the massive, boldly carved head of João I, which is in contrast to the small head and long slender neck of the queen.

The great chest of white limestone resting on the backs of eight lions is decorated on the longest sides with extensive inscriptions in praise of the monarch. The motto of the king – *por bem* (for good) and of the queen – *y me plet* (I love him) are inscribed on the edge of the lid.

The tomb of João I and his queen marked an innovation in medieval Portuguese funerary art, and even though it provided a benchmark for the tomb of their son, Duarte (who succeeded his father), it was never truly emulated.

The most unusual aspect of the tomb is the way in which the king is represented. He is portrayed first and foremost as a military leader, wearing armour and bearing the baton of command, which was fully justified by his victory at Aljubarrota. This is in contrast to the only other royal effigies of which there are remains: the seriously dilapidated figure of King Dinis (1261–1325), which lies in the church of the Convent of Odivelas, and that of Pedro I at the Monastery of Alcobaça, whose dress (a tunic and a long cloak) and unsheathed sword emphasises the power of the king to administer justice. In Portugal at that time it was unheard of to present an effigy of a king or nobleman as a military leader in this way; the fact that this is

Effigies of João I and Philippa of Lancaster in the Founder's Chapel

Tombs of the royal princes in the Founder's Chapel

the case here clearly demonstrates the spirit of innovation which, in various forms, typified the reign of
João I.

In the south wall of the Founder's Chapel, sheltered in arcosolia (recesses) whose architecture closely
follows the aesthetic principles introduced by Huguet elsewhere in the monastery, are the chest tombs
of the royal couple's four sons. These are adorned with their respective crests and coats of arms, including,
in places, the symbols of the English Order of the Garter. This type of funerary monument, like the tomb
of their parents, provided a prototype for tombs at both Santarém and Abrantes.

The first tomb (from left to right) bears the motto *désir* (desire) and belongs to Prince Pedro
(1392–1449), Duke of Coimbra, Lord of Montemor and Aveiro, and regent for King Afonso V before he

Window and 19th-
century tombs in
the Founder's Chapel

came of age. Beside him is his wife Isabel of Aragon, daughter of Jaime, Count of Urgel. Following this is the tomb of Prince Henrique (1394–1460), Duke of Viseu and Lord of Covilhã, Master of the Order of Christ, who became famous as Henry the Navigator, the great patron of Portuguese discoverers. His tomb, which bears the motto *talant de bien fere* (desire to do good) is the only one of the four to bear an effigy that is a replica of his father's, apart from the hands joined in prayer. The next tomb bears the motto *jeai bien resō* (I am in the right) and belongs to Prince João (1400–42), Master of the Order of Santiago and Constable of Portugal. Housed in the same tomb is his wife Isabel (?–1465), daughter of his half-brother Afonso, Duke of Braganza. On the wall above the chest tomb is a relief depicting the Way of the Cross, the Crucifixion and Christ's Descent from the Cross. The fourth tomb, bearing the motto *le bien me plet* (I love what is good), belongs to Prince Fernando (1402–43), Master of the Order of Avis, who died in captivity in the Moroccan city of Fez, and whose bones were brought home after the Portuguese captured Azila in 1471.

According to Luís de Sousa the open niches in the east wall were once occupied by the princes' chapels, each with a small painted altarpiece displaying the patron saint of each prince: the Archangel Michael for Pedro, Prince Fernando (whom he saw as a martyr) for Henrique, John the Baptist for João and Our Lady of the Assumption for Fernando. During the nineteenth-century restorations these were all removed and their contents dispersed. Some religious furnishings disappeared, including João I's altar, which stood at the foot of the royal tomb and acted as a reminder that the Founder's Chapel was a holy place.

On the west wall there were once large cupboards that held liturgical vestments and altar vessels used in each of the prince's chapels. At the end of the nineteenth and the beginning of the twentieth centuries, three imitation fifteenth-century tombs were built there, and the remains of King Afonso V, King João II (1455–95) and João's son Prince Afonso (1475–91), who died on the banks of the Tagus near Santarém, were transferred from the chapter house and the apse-chapel of Our Lady of Mercy. Although at that time the work of the stonemasons was highly regarded, the lack of precision in the execution of the heraldic compositions attracted strong criticism. Some even contended that had the remains of Afonso V, João II and Prince Afonso been moved to King Duarte's pantheon instead of the Founder's Chapel, it might have engendered a more coherent sense of history, since they were all descendents of Duarte, the pantheon's founder.

The large windows on the ground floor and on the second storey of the central octagon, which still retain precious fragments of the original glass, illuminate the entire space with diffuse and translucent light. This creates a sense of seclusion and serenity that transforms the Founder's Chapel from a nostalgic memorial to the dead into a powerful hymn to life and a permanent memorial to the individuals who presided over one of the most brilliant periods in Portugal's history.

Interior of the
Founder's Chapel

THE ROYAL CLOISTER

The Royal Cloister's dimensions (50 x 50 metres) match those of the church, in relation to which it stands on the north side, in line with the tradition of monastic buildings. It is easy to identify the two architects responsible for its construction by examining the various architectural and decorative elements used: vaults, ogees, ribs, column bases and the capitals with their sculpted ornamentation. It is safe to say that the south wing, which backs onto the church, and the east wing, which leads to the chapter house, are the work of the first architect Domingues, in view of the fact that these wings were usually the first to be erected, with work continuing alongside the building of the church itself. The north wing, which leads to the former dormitory, and the west wing, leading to the refectory, were built by the second architect Huguet. Despite the fact that two architects were involved, the final result is perfectly harmonious thanks to the intelligence and sensitivity of Huguet, who oversaw its completion.

The quality of workmanship and the sheer scale of the cloister, which is covered by vaults all the way round, once again confirm João I's intention to celebrate his regal power through the commission of a truly magnificent piece of work. Indeed, in place of the architectural simplicity and restraint that would normally prevail in the monastic cloister of a mendicant order, the splendour and opulence evident here can better be compared to fourteenth-century Portuguese cathedral cloisters, such as those at Oporto

The Royal Cloister before the 19th-century restorations, photograph by Vigé & Plessix, 19th century (Biblioteca da Ajuda)

and Évora cathedrals. The latter, built by Bishop Pedro (d.1340), is perhaps the most accomplished of all for its verticality and its cleverly constructed vault, whose longitudinal ribs connect and unify the central bosses. It is thought that the cloister at Batalha was directly modelled on that of Évora Cathedral, because of the similarity in techniques employed and the overall final result. The cloister at Batalha, like those at Oporto and Évora, is also covered by an easily accessible flat roof.

Practically all the decoration used on the capitals and ceiling bosses consists of plant motifs, although there are noticeable differences between the designs of Domingues and Huguet. A very heavily restored capital in the south wing shows two pairs of Dominican friars, each pair holding up a large open book. The same theme continues on the next capital, on which two human masks appear surrounded by foliage, also with open books. No doubt this was intended to highlight the value of study (to which the Dominicans attached special importance) and the benefits of reading sacred texts. It also refers specifically to the function of this wing of the Batalha cloister, which was known as the Reading Wing, following the example

Capital on an arcade in the Royal Cloister

Dominican friars in the south wing of the Royal Cloister

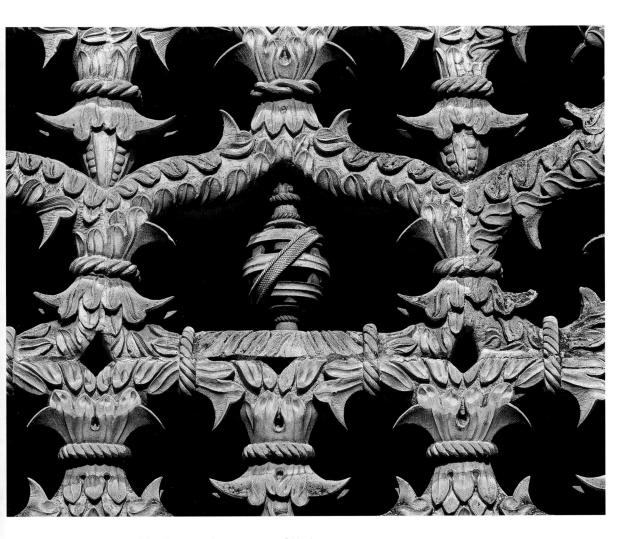

of the cloister at the Monastery of Alcobaça.

At the beginning of the sixteenth century, during the reign of Manuel I, the arcades were filled with magnificent tracery screens resting on slender colonnettes. Together with the Unfinished Chapels, these mark one of the earliest and most significant developments in the gloriously naturalistic art of the Manueline period. The tracery features branches and curving garlands interwoven to form frames for pomegranates and crosses of the Order of Christ. An armillary sphere, discreetly placed on the centre screen on each side of the cloister, marks the midpoint of each side of the square. As well as clearly expressing the power of the monarch, most notably in the central positioning of King Manuel's personal emblem, these exuberant decorations would have made a huge impact, even against the backdrop of what was already a magnificent Royal Cloister.

The armillary sphere, the personal emblem of King Manuel I, on the Manueline tracery screens in the Royal Cloister

Manueline screens in the Royal Cloister arcades

THE CHAPTER HOUSE

Halfway along the cloister's east wing, just after the sacristy, is the door leading to the chapter house – a vast square space of 19 metres on each side.

This room leading off the cloister in a monastery was, after the church, the place where much of the day-to-day activity took place. The governing body (or chapter) met here to review the monastic rules and to discuss issues relating to the life of the community. Along with the church, it was one of the first parts of a monastery to be built and its important function ensured that it was well maintained. The exceptional scale of the chapter house, as well as the technical achievement and aesthetic value inherent in it are evidence of the importance attached to this part of the monastery.

The entrance door is cut into a wall so thick that it is surrounded by five archivolts on the outer side and four on the inside. It is outlined with an openwork trim and flanked, following a custom observed in the Iberian Peninsula since the Romanesque period, by a pair of windows. When seen against the light from the inside, these lend a dramatic sense of fragility to the immense thickness of the wall.

On two capitals to the right of the door is a representation of the Annunciation. The angel on the right has a phylactery (or parchment scroll) hanging from his left shoulder and reaching to his feet, in

Entrance to the chapter house, photograph by Joaquim Augusto Sousa (Museu Vicentes)

Window capitals at the entrance to the chapter house, depicting The Annunciation

accordance with Jewish custom. In place of Old Testament quotations, however, the banner bears the words of the Angel's salutation to Mary. To the angel's right is the Virgin, holding a pitcher in her right hand. Around her neck she wears a necklace with hand-shaped pendants – almost certainly charms to ward off evil. This relatively old-fashioned Marian iconography indicates the work of Domingues. The little human masks surrounded by foliage, which appear on other capitals around the door, can also be attributed to him.

Domingues seems to have intended this vast interior space to be divided into three vaulted naves supported on pillars, like the magnificent chapter house of the Monastery of Alcobaça. However, Domingues died, before the project was completed, and Huguet took over. Although aware of his predecessor's wishes, Huguet opted for a radically innovative solution, choosing to cover the entire space with a single ribbed vault without any central support. Together, the ribs compose a delicate, eight-pointed star with a huge central boss bearing the coat of arms of the king – another sign indicating the supremacy of João I.

The ground-breaking design of this type of vault, both from a technical and an aesthetic viewpoint, is a clear demonstration of Huguet's capabilities. It may also be an indication that Huguet felt a need to assert himself as the man in charge, following Domingues. It might even be argued that the audacity and originality of Huguet's work persuaded João I to commission him to design the Founder's Chapel. Here, instead of being obliged to make adjustments, as he had to do in parts of the chapter house, Huguet was able to start afresh on a plan that achieved great unity in its construction.

Inside the chapter house, on one of the corbels supporting the ribs of the vault, is the figure of the architect. Crouching in the corner to provide better support, he holds in his hand the ruler that is the mark of his profession, and wears a belted tunic and a chaperon (the turban-like headdress fashionable in the

Interior of the chapter house

The Architect,
on a corbel in
the chapter house

fifteenth century). This type of portrait, which also appears in other European countries, clearly indicates the growing social status of the master mason. The presence of the portrait in the chapter house signifies an appreciation of the challenge involved in creating a vault of this type.

On the east wall is a spectacular window with three lights and a tall panel filled with a delicate Flamboyant composition. Like a triptych, the stained-glass panes, dating from 1514, show three scenes from the Crucifixion.

The vast dimensions of the chapter house, with light entering through only one (albeit large) window, mean that the area is always shrouded in semi-darkness. This, along with the subdued colours and sombre subject matter of the window, intensify the air of solemnity. This was reason enough for the Portuguese nation to select it as the place to honour its war dead: since 9 April 1921, the remains of two unknown soldiers of the First World War have lain here.

THE MONKS' DORMITORY (FRIARS' WINE CELLAR) AND THE REFECTORY

Occupying almost the entire north side of the cloister is the former Monks' Dormitory, striking for its immense size and bleak austerity. It is covered by a broken barrel vault, supported by mighty arches that accentuate the sombre atmosphere. Apart from a large two-light window in the east wall, the room is lit solely by rectangular openings set high on the wall, creating a formal simplicity that adds to the room's subdued air.

The type of roof chosen for this building was dictated partly by cost, but it is also a technically traditional one. The choice of roof may also indicate that João I was indeed considering the idea that monks from the monastery at Alcobaça would be housed at Batalha, as it is of a type that was used and favoured at Alcobaça. At the same time the dormitory was designed as a communal area and, as such, would have been inappropriate for Dominican friars, whose way of life was better suited to living in individual cells. Therefore it is not surprising that plans were made to build another cloister (the Afonso V Cloister), with cells along each side. As soon as the new cloister was completed, the former dormitory came to fulfil a different function altogether: it was used as a wine store and is still known today as the Friars' Wine Cellar.

Detail of the basin
of the lavabo in the
Royal Cloister

The last building adjacent to the Royal Cloister is the refectory, which runs the length of the west wing. It is preceded by the lavabo, a small square with a fountain in the middle, set in the angle between the west and north wings. The presence of water here has both ritual and symbolic value, since the washing of hands before entering the refectory was regarded as a symbol of clean living and a pure heart. The lavabo, therefore, was seen as an important area, which explains why, despite its small size, it is a place of considerable beauty, befitting a monastery such as Batalha.

The refectory is similar to the dormitory in its spaciousness and austerity. It is also covered by a broken barrel vault whose pendentives are, however, much slimmer than most of those in the dormitory. And, like the dormitory, it is illuminated by windows placed high above the ground.

Following monastic tradition a pulpit was set into the western wall. At mealtimes a monk would deliver readings from there about the lives of saints and martyrs. On the screen, which is a replica of the original, the armorial bearings of King Duarte and Queen Leonor de Aragon are carved. This is not only a declaration that the pulpit was acquired through the patronage of the royal couple but it may also indicate that the dormitory – where the different treatment of the pendentives marks a change of style –, and the entire construction of the refectory took place during their reign. João I's will seems to confirm this; in it he decreed that 'the cloister, living quarters and all other buildings be completed', which suggests that in 1426, seven years before his death, the cloisters and various other parts of the monastic complex were still unfinished.

In 1924, after the monument to the Unknown Soldier was created in the chapter house, the refectory was adapted to house the present League of Combatants Museum.

Vaulted ceiling
above the lavabo in
the Royal Cloister

THE AFONSO V CLOISTER

Backing onto the north side of the Royal Cloister is a second cloister which, although smaller (44 x 50 metres), is built on a similar ground plan, with seven sections on each side. The Afonso V Cloister is attributed to Fernão de Évora, the architect in charge of the monastery between 1448 and 1477.

The emblems of Afonso V (King of Portugal at the time) on the ground floor ceiling bosses confirm the monarch's patronage and explain the cloister's name. The building of a second cloister began whilst work initiated by João I was still unfinished because the Dominicans needed various facilities, including individual cells, study rooms, a library and storage spaces. These may not have been included in the plans drawn up under João I, or at least no final decisions seem to have been made about providing them at that time.

The most novel feature of the Afonso V Cloister is that it has two storeys. Cloisters were traditionally built on one level, and this was the first time in Portugal that this typical monastic structure took on a new form. The idea may have come from buildings in the region around Barcelona, where two- and even three-storey monastery cloisters were relatively common during the fourteenth and fifteenth centuries. Other features of the Afonso V Cloister also suggest the architectural influence of other areas: the eight-sided colonnettes with capitals stripped of decoration, and the upper-floor configuration of wooden ceilings and beams supported by an architrave on colonnettes, are recurring features in Catalonia.

The ground floor, along which the monastery's various workrooms were laid out, is covered by simple rib vaults which, like the pendentives, rest solely on conical corbels. The lack of vertical colonnettes gives an impression of space and accentuates the horizontal line of the vaulted ceiling. The ceiling bosses, which bear the royal coat of arms and the personal emblem of Afonso V, are the only decorative elements to relieve the starkness of the cloister.

The four sides of the upper storey are lined with individual cells. The simplicity of the wooden ceiling is intensified by the rows of eight-sided colonnettes bearing the architrave supporting the beams. The entirely unadorned capitals eloquently underline the sense of austerity here.

The simplicity of the Afonso V Cloister does not detract from its merits when compared to its opulent neighbour, the Royal Cloister. The latter, in all its architectural and artistic richness and variety, represents a point of arrival, while the former represents a point of departure. Practically every cloister built in Portugal after this time had two storeys and, in some cases, a second storey would be added to an existing cloister, following very closely on the structural and aesthetic pattern set at Batalha.

The simplicity and sense of seclusion of the Afonso V Cloister lend it a profoundly mystical air, in keeping with the original purpose for which it was built. The cloister was at the heart of the monastery, with all the elements essential to the life of the community, including the church, centred around it. At the same time it embodied the ascetic principles that the monks lived by. Here they could commune with God through the beauty and splendour of nature itself, represented by the patch of open sky above the cloister.

The mystical air which remains evident in the Afonso V Cloister today also reflects the movement for religious renewal which was spreading across Europe and into Portuguese society during the fifteenth century. The structure, probably dictated by the Dominican friars, not only displays a new, forward-looking functionality (visible especially in the two-storey elevation) but also indicates the way in which monastic orders focused on the virtues of poverty and austerity advocated by many fifteenth-century Christians.

THE UNFINISHED CHAPELS

The Unfinished Chapels, also known as the Pantheon of King Duarte, consist of an octagonal building situated behind the chancel. It is in perfect alignment with the church, with the entrance on the axis and seven chapels, separated by small triangular partitions, radiating outwards.

Work on the pantheon was commissioned by King Duarte and began some time in 1434, during the first year of his reign. At that time his father João I's funerary chapel had been completed and, according to the late king's will, it was intended to be the burial place of his children and grandchildren. Nevertheless, the new monarch decided to build a new chapel, no less grand than his father's. The fact that he made and implemented this decision after only one year on the throne points to a need on his part to assert himself and his family. Moreover, even though Duarte was king in his own right, and not merely a monarch's son, he may have felt that to be buried among João I's four other sons in the Founder's Chapell would not allow him the prominence he felt he deserved. This may also explain why he chose an octagon with seven equal chapels, even though the building was centrally planned, as was usual in mausoleums; the arrangement he opted for meant that the difference in status between the king and the princes that

Design for the completion of the Unfinished Chapels, by James Murphy, 1795 (Biblioteca e Arquivo Histórico das Obras Publicas)

was exemplified in the Founder's Chapel – where the king's tomb was placed in the centre, and those of the princes were set up close against the wall – could be played down.

Huguet was the architect responsible for the design and construction of the pantheon. At the height of his technical and artistic powers, which had been honed by many years spent in charge of the site at Batalha, he pushed to the limit the plan that had been drawn up for the audacious vault in the chapter house and later adapted for the Founder's Chapel. In terms of innovation the project for the building of the pantheon at Batalha was way ahead of others that were being undertaken in the Iberian Peninsula at that time, including the funerary chapels of Álvaro de Luna and Alonso de Cartagena in Toledo Cathedral, and the Capilla del Condestable (or Constable's Chapel) in Burgos Cathedral.

The death of King Duarte in 1438, after only five years on the throne, and the demise one year later of

Huguet, meant that the new funerary chapel remained unfinished. Unfortunately it is impossible to envisage exactly what the vault that Huguet would have constructed as the ultimate challenge of his career might have looked like.

So it was that, for a variety of reasons, the building remained incomplete for many years. It was not until the beginning of the sixteenth century that Manuel I made plans to complete the pantheon, under the direction of Mateus Fernandes. But even this renewed stage in the chapels' construction, despite being a brilliant moment in the history of Manueline art, was never completed. The king decided instead to lend his patronage to the Jerónimos Monastery in Lisbon. In his will, dated 7 April 1517, he attempted to pass on to his successor the responsibility for completing the work at Batalha which he himself had abandoned: 'I beseech and recommend that he order that the chapels at Batalha be completed as he may see fit and that King Duarte who began the work, and also King Afonso my uncle and King Joam whom God protect and Prince Afonso my nephew be moved there.'

The Renaissance balcony above the entrance, dated 1533 and attributed to João de Castilho, is evidence that Manuel's successor João III (1502–57) did indeed attempt to fulfil his father's wishes. Unfortunately he too abandoned the project, leaving the Duarte's cherished chapels forever unfinished, or as they are known in Portuguese, *imperfeitas* (imperfect).

It is not known whether the original plan included a link to the east end of the church to make it easier for the Dominican friars to perform their daily rituals and to celebrate the anniversaries of those buried there. Nevertheless, it was one of the tasks undertaken by Manuel I, who commissioned the passageway between the church's east end and the entrance to the Unfinished Chapels. The result was a lofty, vaulted

Renaissance gallery, dated 1533, in the Unfinished Chapels

vestibule that was completed in 1509. According to instructions contained in King Manuel's will, this should have continued as far as the church, but his successor never completed the project. In any case, the knowledge that Manuel intended this space to be enclosed or, more probably, that it should directly link one or more of the apse-chapels, helps to explain the significance of the portal of the Unfinished Chapels. Although its dimensions were huge (nearly 15 metres high and 7.5 metres wide) and its interior and exterior opulently decorated, the very sumptuousness of the sculpture meant it was too fragile to support the addition of wooden doors. So it became a triumphal arch in celebration of Portuguese royalty, and in particular of King Manuel I, who had succeeded to the throne through a series of fortuitous and favourable events. King Duarte's motto – *leauté faray* (I will be true) – appears high on the arch and is repeated three times between interwoven branches. The other half of the motto – *tā ya serey* (as long as

Detail of the base of
the triumphal arch in
the Unfinished Chapels

Details of decoration on the triumphal arch in the Unfinished Chapels, drawing by James Murphy, 1795 (Biblioteca e Arquivo Histórico das Obras Publicas)

I shall live), surrounded by wreaths of ivy and repeated more than two hundred times in a sequence that runs along the sculpted columns, follows the curve of the arches, climbing to the highest point of the vaults and descending to the foot of the pillars. This can be seen as a clear sign of Manuel's respect for his predecessor, whose idea it was to construct the pantheon. However, at the top of the arch, on the intrados, are his own emblems (the royal coat of arms, the armillary sphere and the Cross of the Order of Christ), which serve as the ultimate reminder of his authority.

The triumphal arch, or rather the complex series of trefoil arches that provides access to the Unfinished Chapels, was also the work of Fernandes. From the outside, only the first arch has an elaborate outline, like a huge celebratory structure through which the rich decorations on the portal can be glimpsed. On the inside, the artist confined himself to interweaving a polycentric and a trefoil arch.

The remarkable features of this triumphal arch combine to make it one of the most creative and perhaps the greatest example of Manueline art: the complex work on its bases, the differing mouldings on the arcades, the refined and varied decoration (including ivy, artichokes, garlands and motifs suggesting

View of the inner side
of the triumphal arch in
the Unfinished Chapels

woven cloth or basketry), and the alternation of high and low relief creating dramatic contrasts of light and shade. Inside are four empty niches devoid of images but containing miniature corbels and canopies, like architectural models carved with extraordinary technical skill.

At various times vaults were added to the chapels in King Duarte's pantheon, where Huguet had only got as far as building the tracery-edged broken arches. Some of them were probably the work of Fernandes. Resorting to a complex architectural vocabulary, most noticeably in the use of pendants in the English Perpendicular style, the most elaborate of the chapels was the one reserved for King João II and his wife Leonor (1458–1525), who probably commissioned it. Identified by the coats of arms of the king (the pelican tearing at its breast) and the queen (the shrimping net), the dense and elaborate work on the vaulted ceiling above the chapel places it alongside the portal as one of the most original works of Manueline art.

King Manuel's attempt to complete the rotunda included a richly decorated frieze consisting of two parallel mouldings which, in each corner, display the coat of arms of the king laid to rest there. Once again the powerful and eloquent symbolism of heraldry is used to impose the personality of the monarch. The

message is completed by the initials **M**(anuel) and **R**(ex) placed amid abundant decorations in the mouldings that rise from the large windows which would have occupied the upper level of this funerary rotunda.

The roof was never added, and this grandiose space has remained open to the sky. The absence of a roof has given rise to a variety of suggestions for the completion of the building, such as those of a German architect visiting Portugal in the late nineteenth century who had the idea that the building should be completed in the style of an Indian temple...

Only at the beginning of the twentieth century was the double tomb of King Duarte and Queen Leonor finally placed here in the axial chapel. The couple are holding hands, in imitation of the figures on the tomb of King João I and Philippa of Lancaster.

The transfer from its previous position at the entrance to the chancel of the church marked, at least symbolically, the completion of the pantheon that Duarte had dreamed of. It was the King's final encounter with history.

Detail of the base of the triumphal arch in the Unfinished Chapels

Royal coat of arms in the vault above the chapel in the Unfinished Chapels, intended to hold the tombs of King João II and Queen Leonor

Joint tomb of King Duarte and Queen Leonor in the Unfinished Chapels

THE WINDOWS

Work on the stained-glass windows at the Batalha Monastery began somewhere between the late 1430s and the early 1440s, and it is believed to have been the first building in Portugal to be decorated in this way. Of the original windows there remain fragments of figurative compositions, decorative plant motifs and geometric figures, as well as a large number of panes of heraldic glass. According to Luís de Sousa's description of the monastery from around 1623, the windows in the church and the Founder's Chapel were still intact at that time.

Mousinho de Albuquerque, who first took charge of restorations at the monastery in late 1840, described the advanced state of disrepair of the windows. He then outlined the methods he used to restore them, although much of the original glass had already been lost by then. In the windows along the side aisles there were vestiges of the original glass, which were removed, dismantled and then reassembled in new lead cames (or grooved strips) to form small panes which sometimes contained pieces of the original glass. These new panes were then placed halfway up large wooden frames containing coloured glass. In the absence of any concrete plan for the windows, the intention was to evoke an atmosphere of a long-lost past.

The fragments that Mousinho placed in the large wooden frames in the side aisles were taken down and treated between 1996 and 2005, and due to their dilapidated state they were not returned to their original location. Even so, they remain the earliest proof of the existence of stained-glass windows at the

Original glass (15th or 16th century)

Glass replaced or installed in the 19th century

Original glass or fragment from a different section of the window pane

New cames used in repairs

Main supporting cames

Diagram showing the state of preservation of the pane prior to restoration

Haloed figure, taken from the north aisle of the church, *c.* 1440–80

Monastery of Batalha, and the first of their kind in Portugal. Technically, a stained-glass window is a collection of glass pieces mounted in a framework of lead cames. The glass may be plain or coloured either by adding powdered metals while it is still molten, or sometimes by painting.

The first stained-glass artist known to have worked at Batalha was Luís Alemão. He arrived at the monastery from his native southern Germany in the late 1430s or early 1440s. The most ancient windows of the monastery share many characteristics with those found in Nuremberg and other parts of the Franconia region in southern Germany.

Some of the fifteenth-century windows are fashioned in the same basic style as these, but the figures

The oldest windows show prophets with closed or open scrolls portrayed as patriarchs, saints or angels. Others show scenes from the life of Christ or related to His death and resurrection.

Some 15th-century glass shares the same basic style as earlier examples, although the figures – painted with much greater refinement on large areas of plain glass – are more elegant.

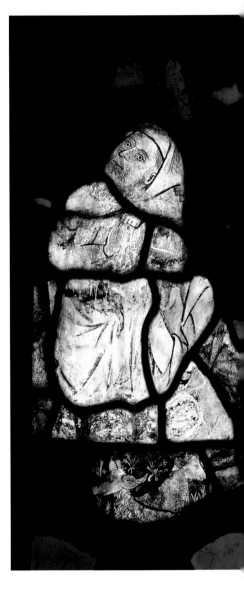

are more elegant and are painted with greater refinement on large areas of plain glass.

The similarities between these works and those surviving in Nuremberg indicates that a new artist, a compatriot of Luís Alemão, came to work at Batalha in the middle of the fifteenth century.

Fragment showing the Annunciation to the shepherds of the birth of Jesus: 'And there were in the same country shepherds abiding in the field, keeping watch over their flocks by night. And, lo, the angel of the Lord came unto them and they were sore afraid'. Luke 2: 8-9

In the first decade of the 15th century, the quest for realism went hand-in-hand with far-reaching changes in painting techniques. One of the artists involved was Master João, believed to be Flemish, to whom these fragments of The Last Supper (1508) are attributed.

Portraits of King Manuel and his second wife, Maria, with their children and two Dominican saints

Standard bearers carrying the Cross of the Order of Christ and the armillary sphere, in the chancel of the church, *c.* 1514

In the second decade of the sixteenth century, King Manuel commissioned complete sets of stained-glass windows for the chancel of the church and the chapter house. These exemplify the authority of the royal family, represented by portraits of its members and their coats of arms, and the power of the Dominican Order, which had close associations with the monarchy. The windows were designed and the glass painted by artists skilled at painting on canvas. They included Manuel's court painter, Francisco Henriques, whose signature appears on the Pentecost scene.

The painter Francisco Henriques chose to place his signature in the bottom right-hand corner of this representation of St John the Baptist. He would turn to the same biblical subject when the king commissioned him to paint the altarpieces for the church of São Francisco at Évora (1509–11).

During the fifteenth and sixteenth centuries the Monastery of Batalha became Portugal's main centre for the creation of stained glass. Practically everyone who practised the art spent time here before moving on to other parts of the country to take on various commissions, many of them for the king himself.

In the 1870s stained glass was produced again at Batalha, this time by the restorers of the monastery. They started the process of replacing original stained glass with coloured glass in wooden frames.

The stained-glass windows in the chapter house, dated 1514, were probably designed by Francisco Henriques, although they were painted by another, unknown artist. Like the windows in the chancel, those in the chapter house are intended to be a large altarpiece, in this case a triptych depicting scenes from The Passion.

The Virgin enthroned with the Christ Child (above and right) dates from the late 1520s or early 1530s. It differs from the other chancel windows in the somewhat theatrical poses of the figures, the subtle, edgy painting style and the classical characteristics of the throne. It was probably the work of Pero Picardo, a native of Picardy, a region north of Paris and bordering Flanders, where windows with identical characteristics dating from the same period can be found.

The General Directorate for Buildings and National Monuments began replacing the wooden frames of some of the windows in the nave in the early 1930s, engaging the Lisbon specialist firm of Ricardo Leone to undertake the work. This project was interrupted in 1931 when restoration of the chapter house windows began, and was never resumed.

Following page
Windows on the second storey of the chancel

BIBLIOGRAPHY

ALBUQUERQUE, Luís da Silva Mousinho de, *Memória inédita àcerca do edifício monumental da Batalha,* Leiria, Tip. Leiriense, 1854.

ANDRADE, Sérgio Guimarães de, *Mosteiro da Batalha,* Lisbon, Instituto Português do Património Cultural, 1989.

BARROS, Carlos Vitorino da Silva, *O Vitral em Portugal, Séculos XV e XVI,* Lisbon, Comissariado para a XVII Exposição Europeia de Arte, Ciência e Cultura, 1983.

CHICÓ, Mário Tavares, *Remarques sur le choeur de l'église de Sainte-Marie de la Victoire (Batalha),* Lisbon, 1940.

CHICÓ, Mário Tavares, *Arquitectura da Idade Média em Portugal. Dois Estudos acerca da Igreja do Mosteiro da Batalha,* Lisbon, Instituto para a Alta Cultura, 1944.

CHICÓ, Mário Tavares, *A Arquitectura Gótica em Portugal,* 3rd edition, Lisbon, Livros Horizonte, 1981.

CORREIA, Vergílio, *Batalha, Estudo Historico-Artistico-Arqueologico do Mosteiro da Batalha,* Oporto, Litografia Nacional, 1929.

CORREIA, Vergílio, *Batalha – II, Estudo Histórico-Artístico da Escultura do Mosteiro da Batalha,* Oporto, Litografia Nacional, 1931.

GOMES, Saul António, *O Mosteiro de Santa Maria da Vitória no Século XV,* Coimbra, Instituto de História da Arte - Faculdade de Letras da Universidade de Coimbra, 1990.

GOMES, Saul António, *Vésperas Batalhinas, Estudos de História e Arte,* Leiria, Edições Magno, 1997.

GOMES, Saul António, *Fontes Históricas e Artísticas do Mosteiro e da Vila da Batalha (Séculos XIV a XVII).* Vol. I, Lisbon, Instituto Português do Património Arquitectónico (IPPAR), 2002.

HESS, Daniel, 'In search of Luis Alemão: Stained Glass in Germany from 1400 to 1460 and the fragments in Batalha', in *O Vitral, História, Conservação e Restauro,* Lisbon, Instituto Português do Património Arquitectónico (IPPAR), 2002, pp. 44-53.

MURPHY, James C., *Plans, Elevations, Sections and Views of the Church of Batalha in the Province of Estremadura in Portugal,* London, I. J. Taylor, 1795.

MURPHY, James C., *Viagens em Portugal,* (original edition: *Travels in Portugal,* 1795), Lisbon, Livros Horizonte, 1998.

NETO, Maria João Baptista, 'O Restauro do Mosteiro de Santa Maria da Vitória de 1840 a 1900', in *Cadernos de História da Arte,* Lisbon, Instituto de História da Arte/Faculdade de Letras de Lisbon, 1991.

NETO, Maria João Baptista, *James Murphy e o Restauro do Mosteiro de Santa Maria da Vitória no Século XIX,* Lisbon, Editorial Estampa, 1997.

PEREIRA, Paulo, *James Murphy e o Mosteiro da Batalha,* Lisbon, Instituto Português do Património Cultural, 1989.

REDOL, Pedro, *O Mosteiro da Batalha e o Vitral em Portugal nos Séculos XV e XVI,* Lisbon, Câmara Municipal da Batalha, 2003.

SANTOS, Reinaldo dos, *Batalha, Guia de Portugal, II, Extremadura, Alentejo, Algarve,* Lisbon, Biblioteca Nacional de Lisbon, 1927, pp. 669-690.

SÃO LUIZ, Frei Francisco de, 'Memoria Histórica sobre as Obras do Real Mosteiro de Santa Maria da Victoria, chamado vulgarmente da Batalha', in *Obras Completas,* Vols I and X, Lisbon, Imprensa Nacional, 1827.

SILVA, José Custódio Vieira da, *O Tardo-Gótico em Portugal. A Arquitectura no Alentejo,* Lisbon, Livros Horizonte, 1989.

SILVA, José Custódio Vieira da, 'Para um entendimento da Batalha: a influência mediterrânica', in *Actas do III Encontro sobre História Dominicana,* Oporto, Dominicanos, 1991.

SILVA, José Custódio Vieira da, *Arte Gótica, História da Arte Portuguesa, Época Medieval,* Lisbon, Universidade Aberta, 1995.

SILVA, José Custódio Vieira da, 'A Importância da Genealogia e da Heráldica na Representação Artística Manuelina', in *O Fascínio do Fim,* Lisbon, Livros Horizonte, 1997.

SOARES, Clara Moura, *A lavra das pedreiras e o estaleiro das obras de restauro do Mosteiro de Santa Maria da Vitória no século XIX,* Lisbon, Faculdade de Letras-Universidade de Lisbon, Master's Dissertation, 1999.

SOUSA, Frei Luís de, *História de S. Domingos,* Oporto, Lello e Irmão, Editores, 1977.

VITRAIS, *Boletim da Direcção Geral dos Edifícios e Monumentos Nacionais.* No. 118, Lisbon, 1964.